JUST FOR FUN

EASY ROCK UKULELE

12 GREAT ROCK SONGS–JUST A FEW CHORDS

ARRANGED BY BURGESS SPEED AND HEMME LUTTJEBOER

Produced by
Alfred Music Publishing Co., Inc.
P.O. Box 10003
Van Nuys, CA 91410-0003
alfred.com

Printed in USA.

ISBN-10: 0-7390-6461-4
ISBN-13: 978-0-7390-6461-0

Cover Photos
Central image models: Katrina Hruschka and Andrew Callahan / Photographer: Brian Immke, www.adeptstudios.com
3 Cherry uke: courtesy of C. F. Martin & Co • Moon: courtesy of The Library of Congress • Gramophone: © istockphoto / Faruk Tasdemir
MP3 player: © istockphoto / tpopova • Microphone: © istockphoto / Graffizone • Handstand: © istockphoto / jhorrocks
Jumping woman: © istockphoto / Dan Wilton • Woman and radio: courtesy of The Library of Congress • Sneakers: © istockphoto / ozgurdonmaz
Background: image copyright Elise Gravel, 2009, used under license from Shutterstock.com

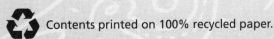
Contents printed on 100% recycled paper.

FOREWORD

Easy Rock Ukulele is designed for your total enjoyment. Each featured song is inherently simple, with just a few chords. All the tunes are arranged for ukulele from the actual guitar parts, simplified just enough to keep them fun and musically satisfying. Make sure to listen to the original recordings so you know how these parts should sound before you start trying to learn them. But most important, just have fun!

—Aaron Stang, Editor
Alfred Music Publishing Co., Inc.

CONTENTS

AS TEARS GO BY

Words and Music by
MICK JAGGER, KEITH RICHARDS
and ANDREW LOOG OLDHAM

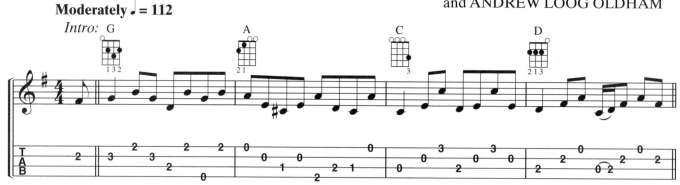

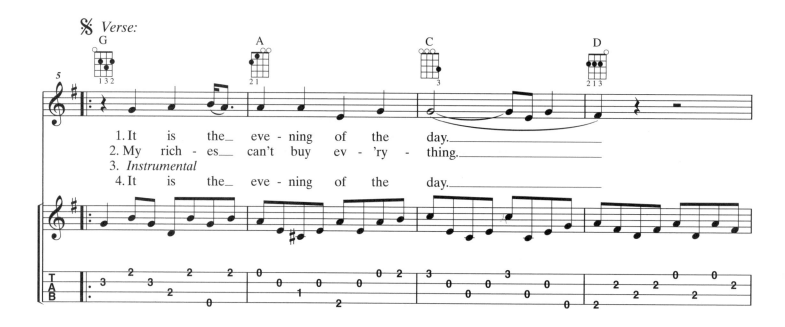

1. It is the_ eve-ning of the day.____
2. My rich-es_ can't buy ev-'ry - thing.____
3. *Instrumental*
4. It is the_ eve-ning of the day.____

I sit and_ watch the_ chil-dren play.____
I want to_ hear the_ chil-dren sing.____
I sit and_ watch the_ chil-dren play.____

As Tears Go By - 2 - 1

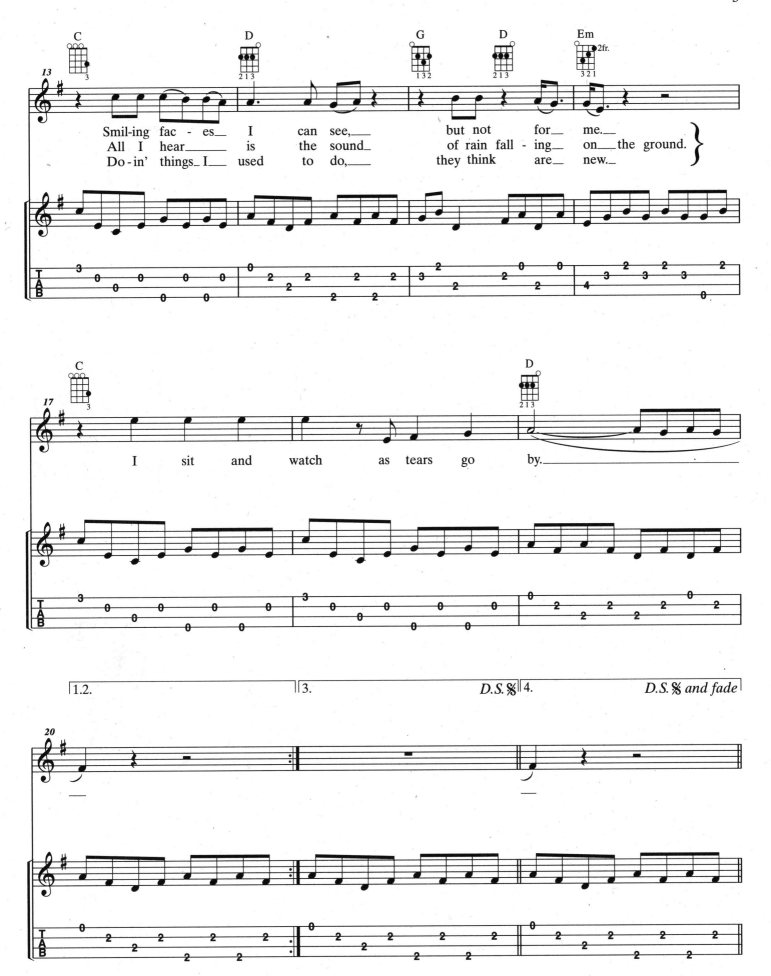

BIG YELLOW TAXI

Words and Music by
JONI MITCHELL

paved par-a-dise,_ put up a park-ing lot.___ With a pink_

2.3.4. *See additional lyrics*

_ ho-tel,_ a bou-tique, and a swing-ing___ hot_ spot.__

Chorus:

Don't it al-ways seem_ to go that you don't know what_ you've got___ till it's gone. They

Big Yellow Taxi - 2 - 1

Verse 2:
They took all the trees,
Put 'em in a tree museum.
And they charged the people
A dollar and a half just to see 'em.
(To Chorus:)

Verse 3:
Hey farmer, farmer,
Put away that DDT now.
Give me spots on my apples,
But leave me the birds and the bees,
Please!
(To Chorus:)

Verse 4:
Late last night
I heard the screen door slam.
And a big yellow taxi
Took away my old man.
(To Chorus:)

CASEY JONES

Words by
ROBERT HUNTER

Music by
JERRY GARCIA

Medium tempo ♩ = 92

Chorus:

Driv-ing that train,__ high on co-caine,__ Ca-sey Jones,__ you'd bet-ter watch your speed.__ Trou-ble a-head,__ trou-ble be-hind,__ and you know that no-tion just crossed my mind.___

Verse:

1. This old en-gine makes it on time,__ leaves Cen-tral Sta-tion 'bout a
2. Trou-ble a-head, the la-dy in red,__ take my ad-vice__ you'd be
3. *Instrumental*
4. *See additional lyrics*

Casey Jones - 2 - 1

Verse 4:
Trouble with you is the trouble with me,
Got two good eyes but you still don't see.
Come 'round the bend, you know it's the end,
The fireman screams and the engine just gleams.
(To Chorus:)

GIMME SOME LOVIN'

Words and Music by
STEVE WINWOOD, MUFF WINWOOD
and SPENCER DAVIS

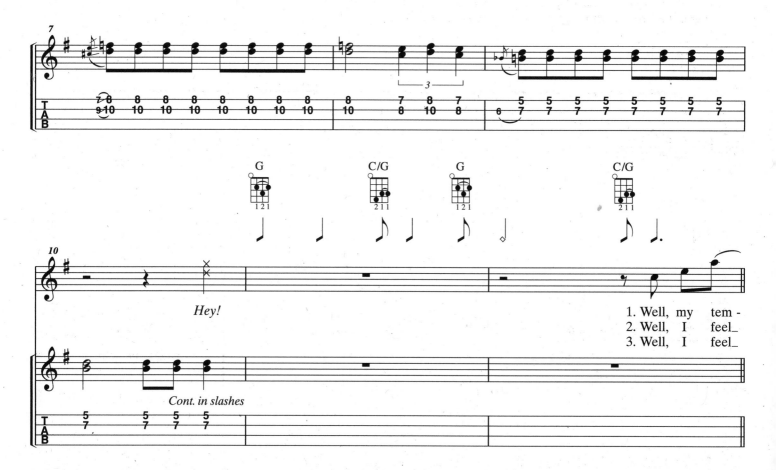

Gimme Some Lovin' - 3 - 1

MARGARITAVILLE

Words and Music by
JIMMY BUFFETT

Margaritaville - 3 - 1

14

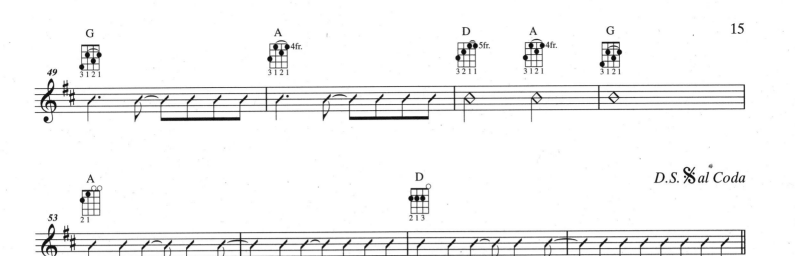

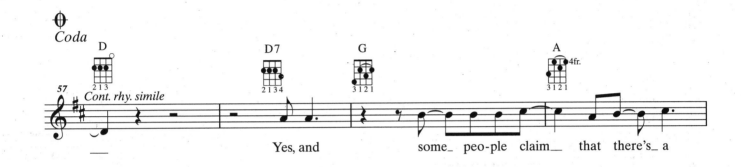

D.S. 𝄋 al Coda

Coda

Yes, and some_ peo-ple claim_ that there's_ a wom - an to blame_____ and I know_ it's my own_ damn_ fault.

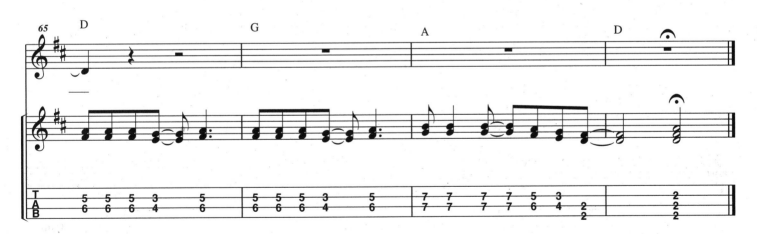

Verse 2:
Don't know the reason,
I stayed here all season
With nothing to show but this brand-new tattoo.
But it's a real beauty,
A Mexican cutie,
How it got here I haven't a clue.
(To Chorus:)

Verse 3:
Old men in tank tops
Cruising the gift shops
Checking out the chiquitas down by the shore.
They dream about weight loss,
Wish they could be their own boss.
Those three-day vacations become such a bore.

Verse 4:
I blew out my flip-flop,
Stepped on a pop-top;
Cut my heel, had to cruise on back home.
But there's booze in the blender,
And soon it will render
That frozen concoction that helps me hang on.
(To Chorus:)

* "Lost" verse (Live version only)

GLORIA

Words and Music by
VAN MORRISON

1. I'd like to tell you 'bout my

ba - by,
2. *See additional lyrics*

you know, she comes a - round.___

Just a-bout five feet four,___

from her head to the ground.___

___ You know,___ she comes a - round here,___

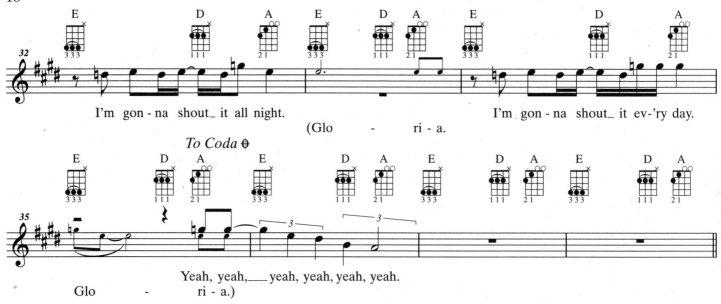

I'm gon - na shout_ it all night.

(Glo - ri - a.

To Coda ⊕

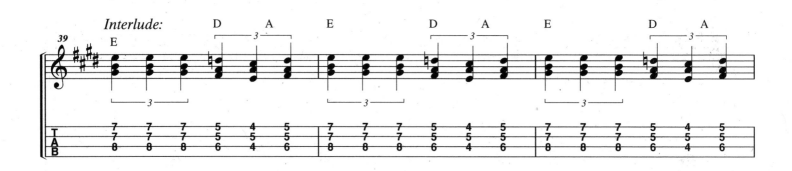

Yeah, yeah,___ yeah, yeah, yeah, yeah.

Glo - ri - a.)

I'm gon - na shout_ it ev-'ry day.

Interlude:

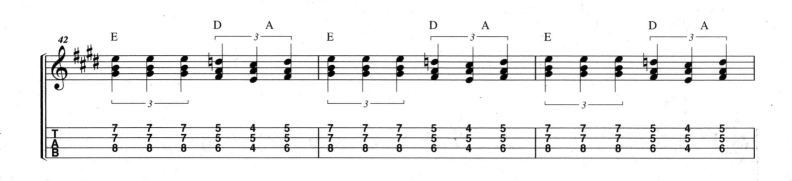

Verse 2: (Half Spoken)
She comes around here
Just about midnight.
She make me feel so good,
I wanna say she make me feel alright.
Comes walkin' down my street,
Watch her come to my house.
She knocks upon my door,
And then she comes to my room.
Then she makes me feel alright,
G-l-o-r-i-a.
(To Chorus:)

MOONDANCE

Words and Music by
VAN MORRISON

Moondance - 3 - 1

TAKE ME HOME, COUNTRY ROADS

Words and Music by
JOHN DENVER, BILL DANOFF
and TAFFY NIVERT

Take Me Home, Country Roads - 3 - 1

GOOD RIDDANCE (TIME OF YOUR LIFE)

Lyrics by
BILLIE JOE

Music by
BILLIE JOE and GREEN DAY

Bright in 2 ♩ = 86

*For ease of use we have not used double noteheads for the unison G notes (open G and 3rd fret G).
Refer to the TAB for the correct fingerings.

Good Riddance (Time of Your Life) - 4 - 1

28

Interlude:

Good Riddance (Time of Your Life) - 4 - 4

A HORSE WITH NO NAME

Words and Music by
DEWEY BUNNELL

A Horse with No Name - 3 - 1

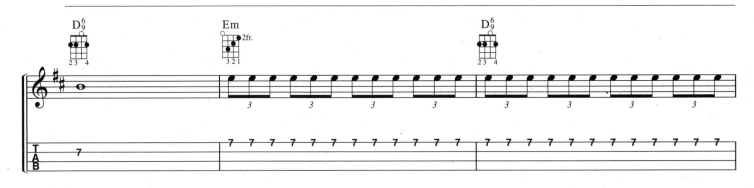

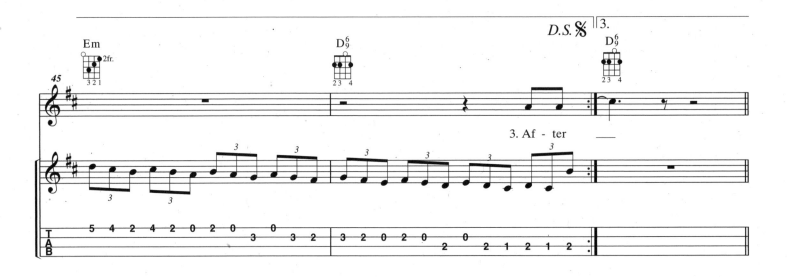

Verse 2:
After two days in the desert sun
My skin began to turn red.
After three days in the desert fun
I was looking at a river bed.
And the story it told of a river that flowed
Made me sad to think it was dead.
You see, I've
(To Chorus:)

Verse 3:
After nine days I let the horse run free
'Cause the desert had turned to sea.
There were plants and birds and rocks and things,
There were sand and hills and rings.
The ocean is a desert with its life underground
And the perfect disguise above.
Under the cities lies a heart made of ground,
But the humans will give no love.
You see, I've
(To Chorus:)

TAKE IT EASY

Words and Music by
JACKSON BROWNE
and GLENN FREY

Moderately ♩ = 138

Intro:

*Unison A notes played
on 1st and 2nd strings
(see TAB).

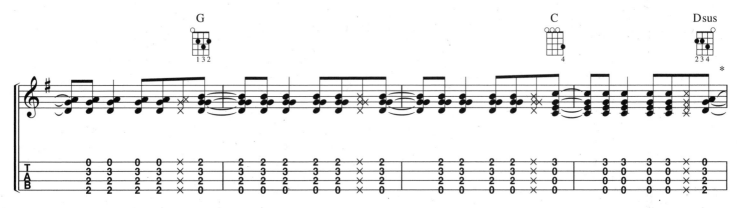

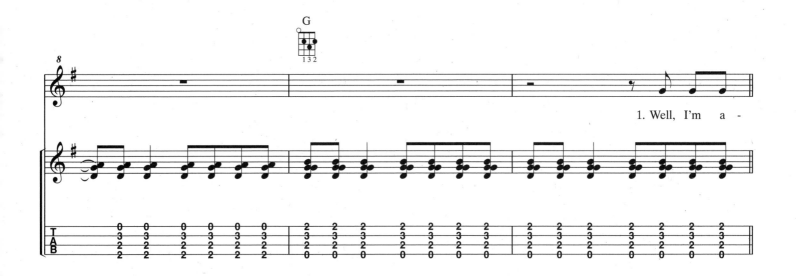

1. Well, I'm a-

Take It Easy - 5 - 1

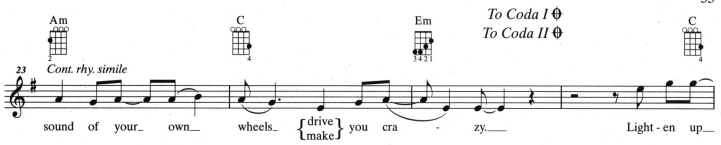

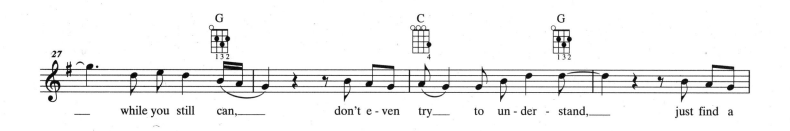

sound of your_ own_ wheels_ {drive / make} you cra - zy._ Light - en up_

_ while you still can,_ don't e - ven try_ to un - der - stand,_ just find a

place to make_ your stand,_ and take it eas - y._

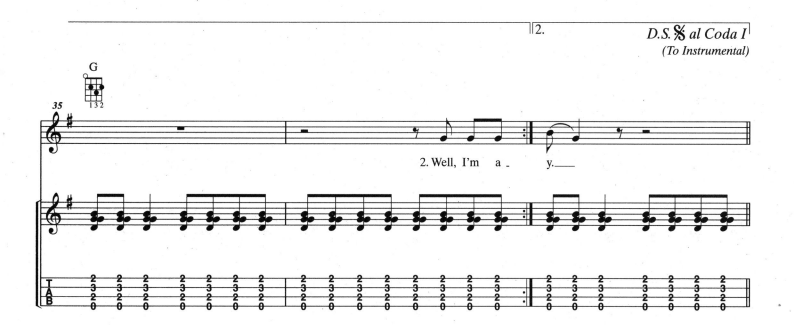

2. Well, I'm a _ y._

Coda I

3. Well,   I'm   a -

Coda II

Come on,__ ba -   by,   don't say__ may -

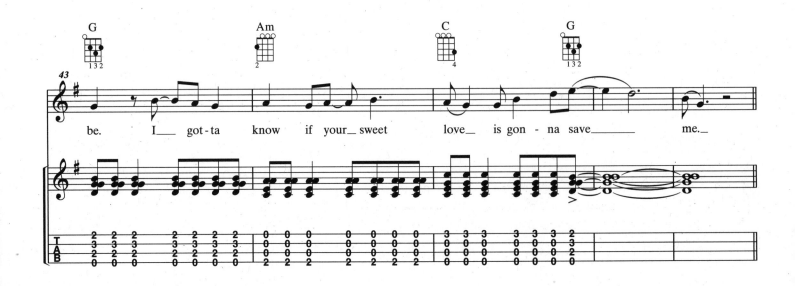

be.   I__ got - ta   know   if your__ sweet   love__ is gon - na save_____   me.__

Outro:

PEACEFUL EASY FEELING

Words and Music by
JACK TEMPCHIN

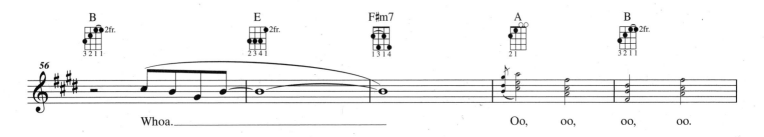

Whoa._____ Oo, oo, oo, oo.

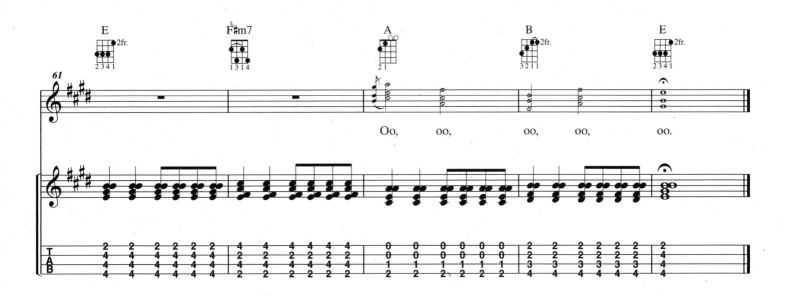

Oo, oo, oo, oo, oo.

Verse 2:
And I found out a long time ago
What a woman can do to your soul.
Ah, but she can't take you anyway,
You don't already know.
(To Chorus:)

Verse 3:
I get this feelin' I may know you
As a lover and a friend.
But this voice keeps whispering in my other ear,
Tells me I may never see you again.
(To Chorus:)

UKULELE CHORD DICTIONARY

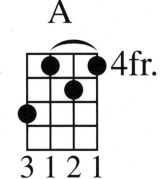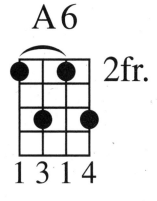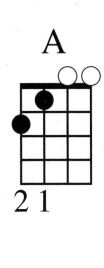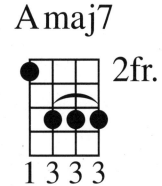

A CHORDS

A

A   4fr.

Amaj7   2fr.

A6   2fr.

2 1

3 1 2 1

1 3 3 3

1 3 1 4

Am

Am   2fr.

Am7

Am6

2

1 3 4 2

2 3

A7

A7

A9

A13

2 1 3

1 3 2 4

1 3

1 2 3

Asus

A7sus

Adim7

A⁺

2 3

2

1 3 2 4

3 1 2

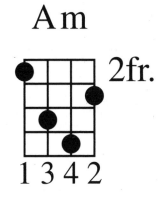
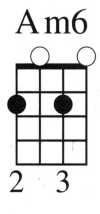
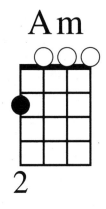
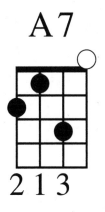
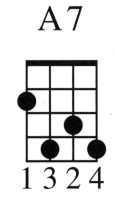
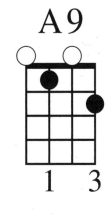
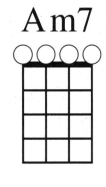
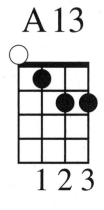
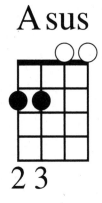
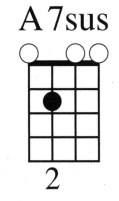
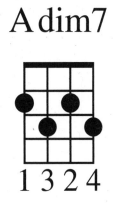
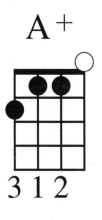

B♭ (A♯) CHORDS*

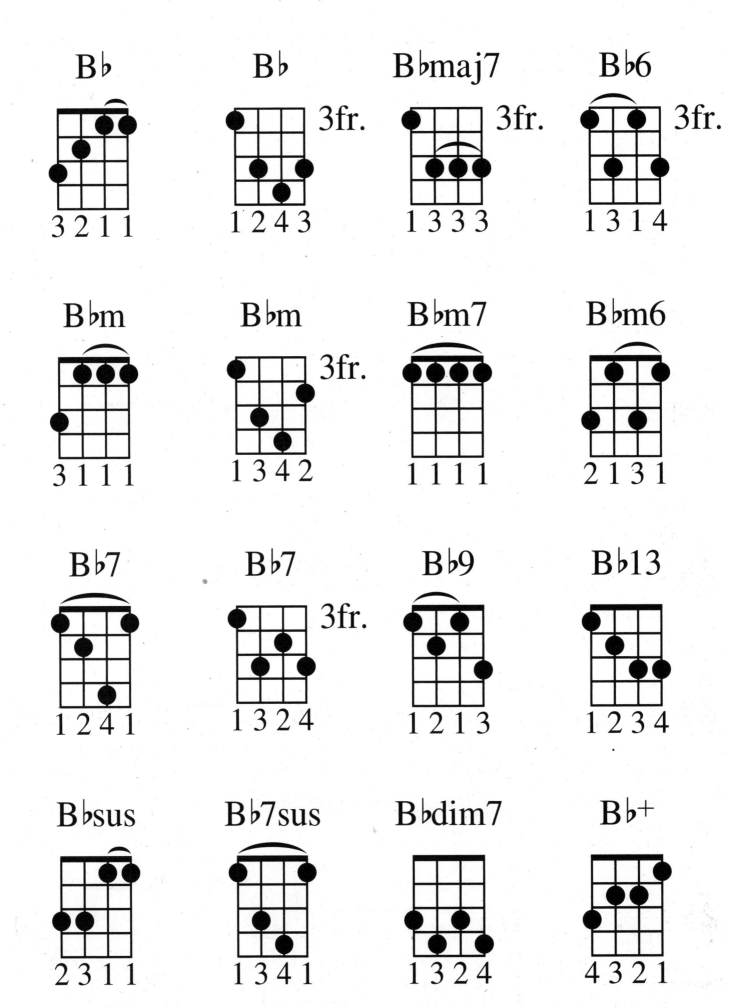

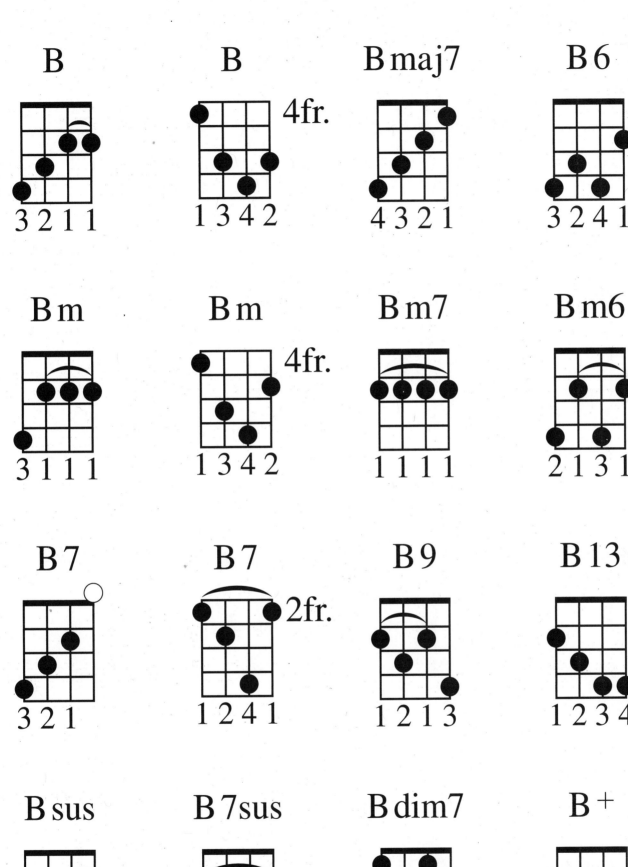

C CHORDS

C
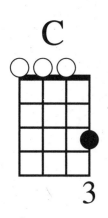
3

C
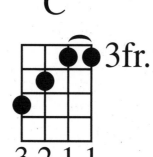 3fr.
3 2 1 1

Cmaj7
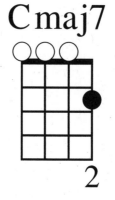
2

C6
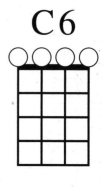

Cm
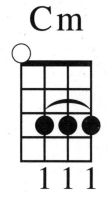
1 1 1

Cm
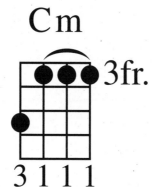 3fr.
3 1 1 1

Cm7
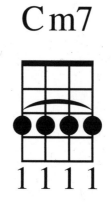
1 1 1 1

Cm6
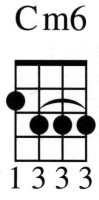
1 3 3 3

C7
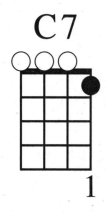
1

C7
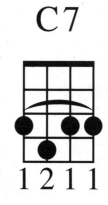
1 2 1 1

C9
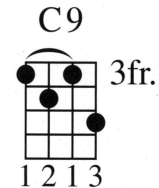 3fr.
1 2 1 3

C13
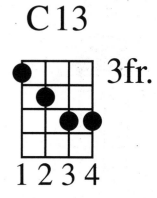 3fr.
1 2 3 4

Csus
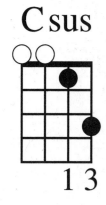
1 3

C7sus
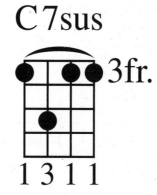 3fr.
1 3 1 1

Cdim7
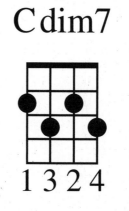
1 3 2 4

C+
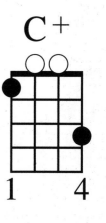
1   4

C♯ (D♭) CHORDS*

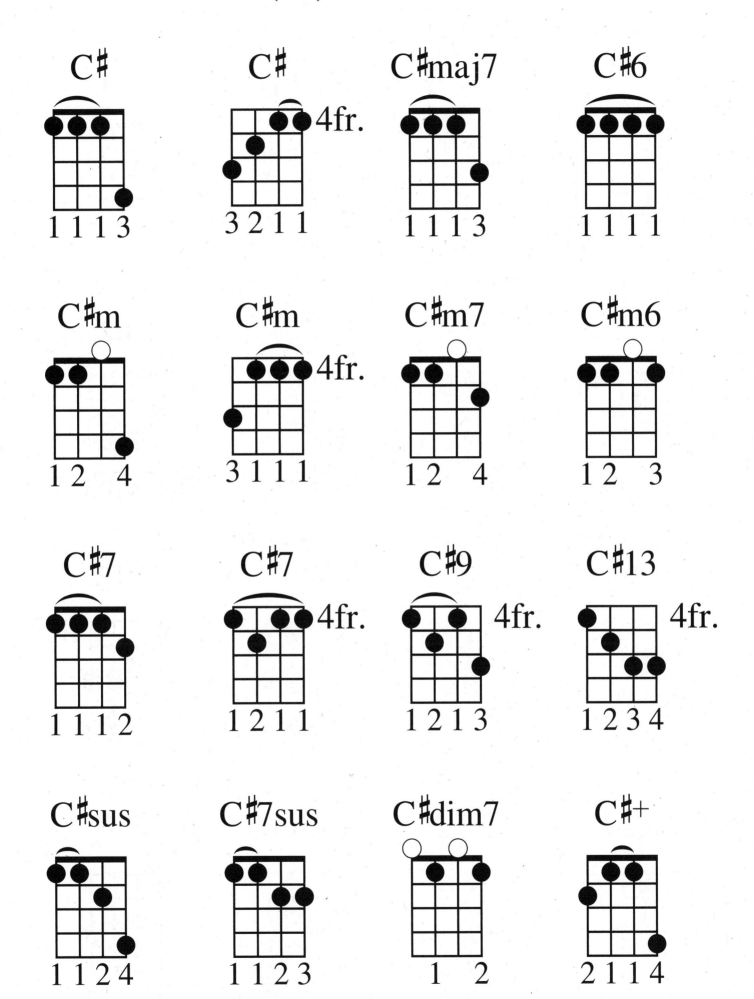

*C♯ and D♭ are two names for the same note.

D CHORDS

D
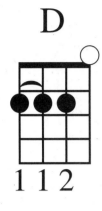
1 1 2

D
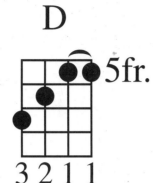
5fr.
3 2 1 1

Dmaj7
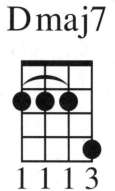
1 1 1 3

D6
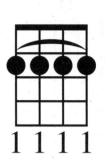
1 1 1 1

Dm
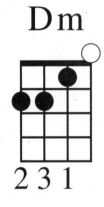
2 3 1

Dm
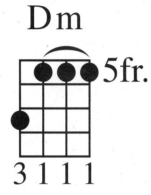
5fr.
3 1 1 1

Dm7
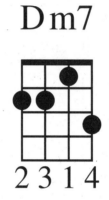
2 3 1 4

Dm6
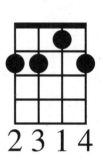
2 3 1 4

D7
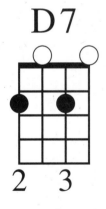
2   3

D7

1 1 1 2

D9
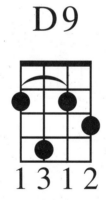
1 3 1 2

D13
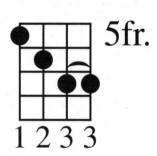
5fr.
1 2 3 3

Dsus
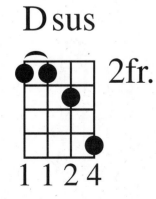
2fr.
1 1 2 4

D7sus
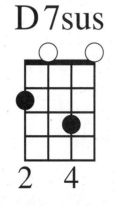
2   4

Ddim7
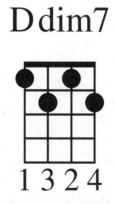
1 3 2 4

D+
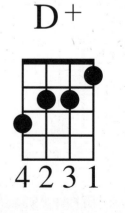
4 2 3 1

E♭ (D♯) CHORDS*

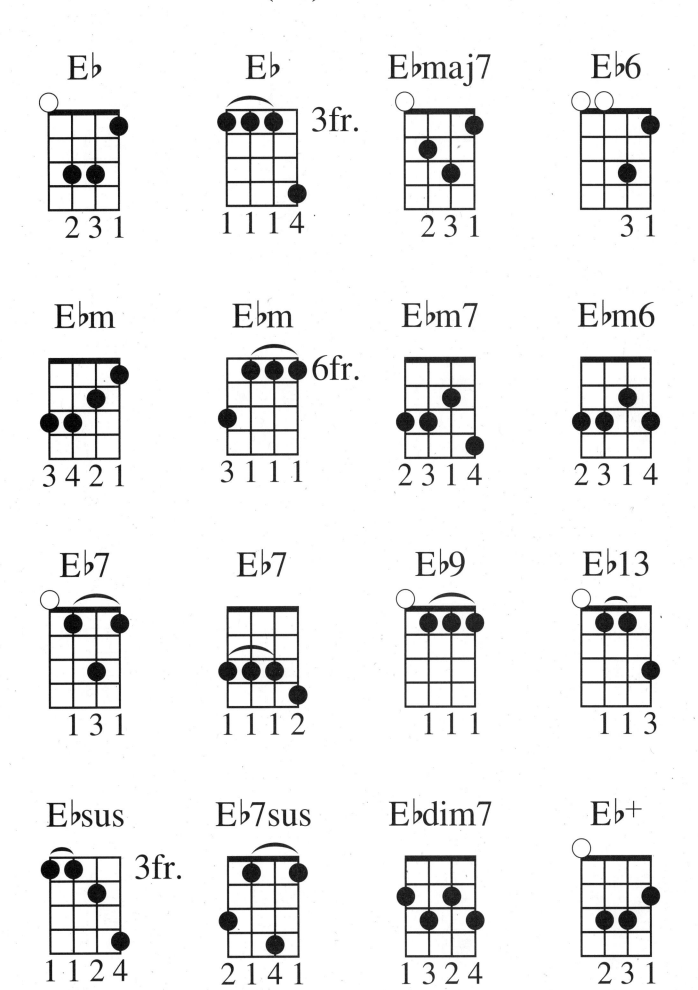

*E♭ and D♯ are two names for the same note.

E CHORDS

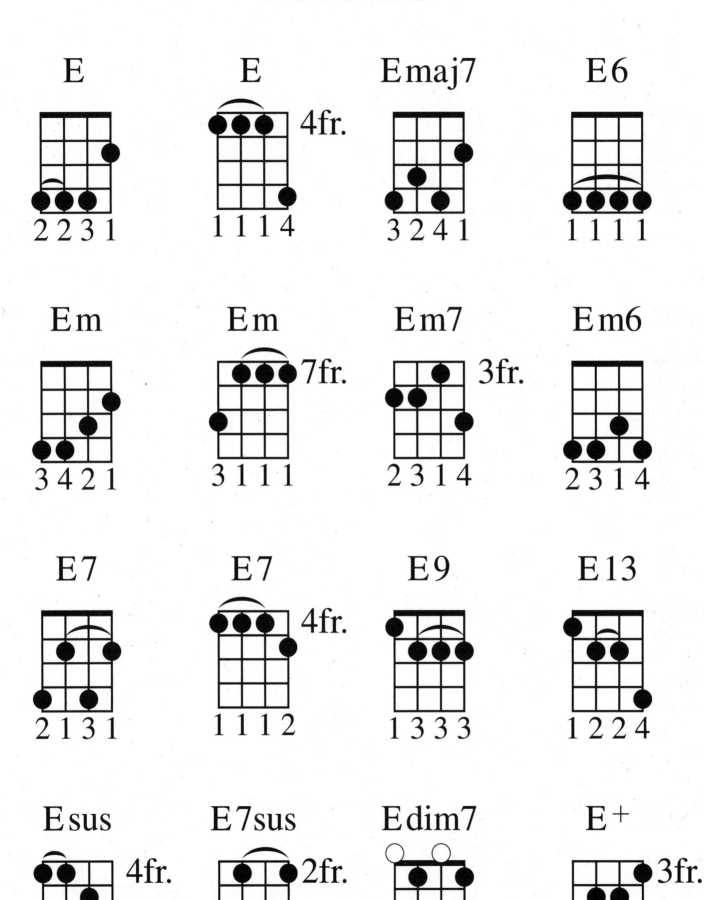

F CHORDS

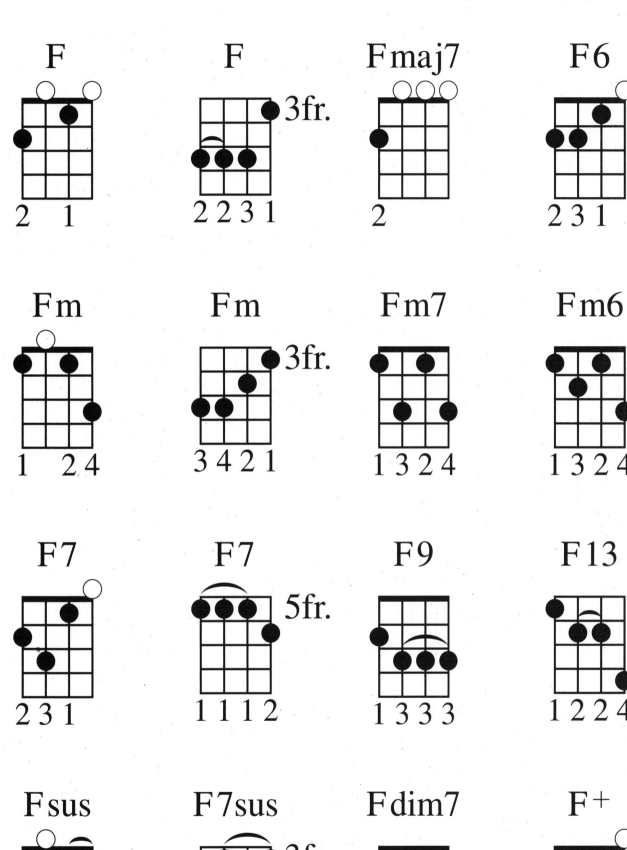

F♯ (G♭) CHORDS*

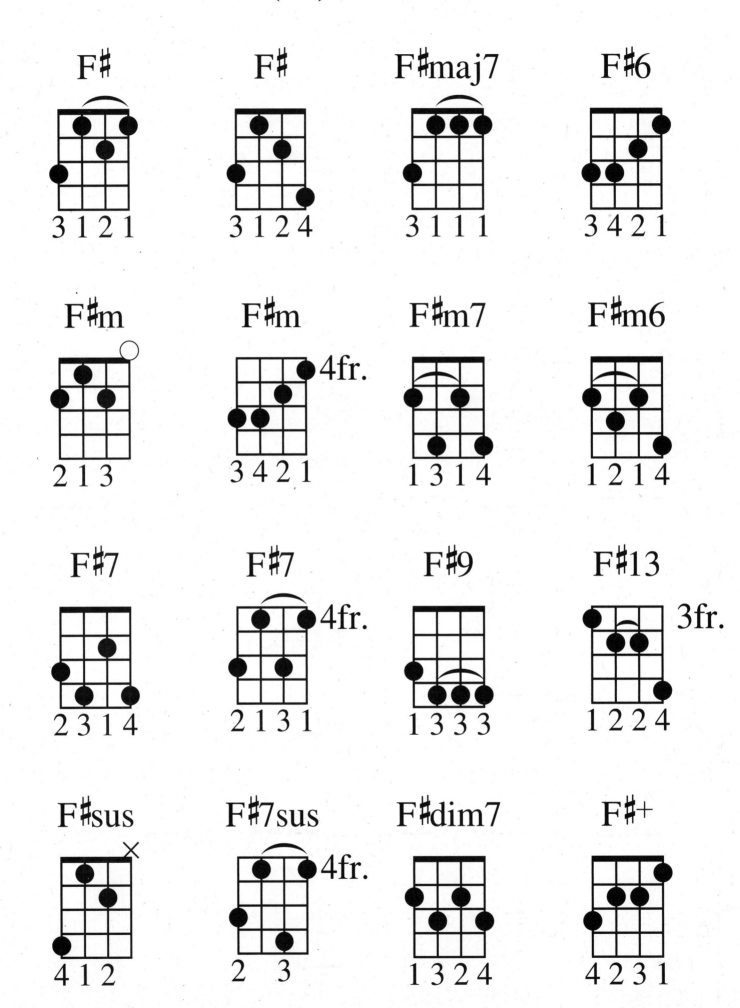

*F♯ and G♭ are two names for the same note.

G CHORDS

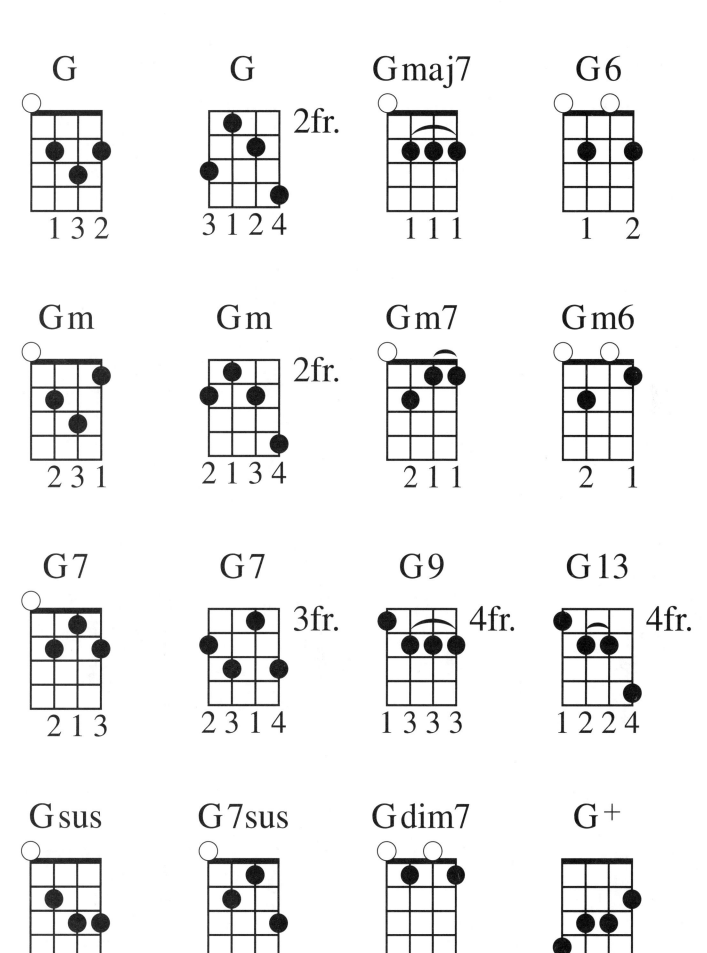

A♭ (G♯) CHORDS

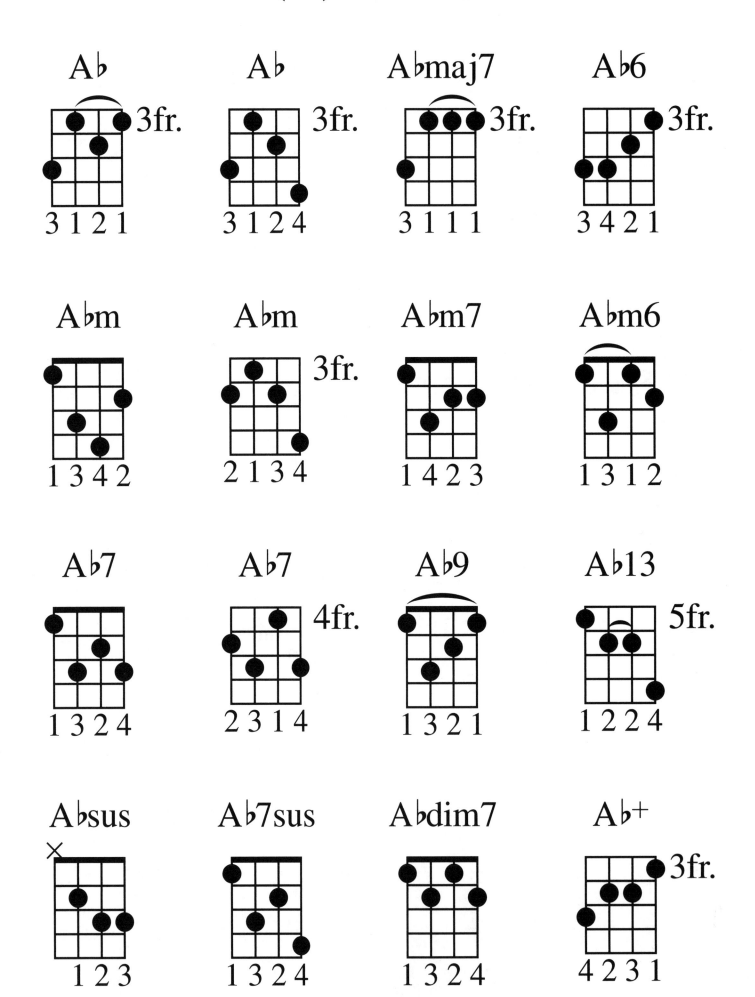

*A♭ and G♯ are two names for the same note.